CONTENTS

WHO WAS JOHN LENNON? 4

EARLY YEARS IN LIVERPOOL 6

THE RISE OF THE BEATLES 12

WORLD FAMOUS 18

THE BUBBLE BURSTS 22

A NEW MARRIAGE AND NEW DIRECTIONS . . .26

THE SWINGING SIXTIES 30

LIFE WITH YOKO 32

LYING LOW 36

THE LAST MONTHS 40

THE LENNON LEGACY 46

CHANGING VIEWS OF JOHN LENNON 50

FILMS, BOOKS AND RECORDS 52

GLOSSARY 54

INDEX 56

WHO WAS JOHN LENNON?

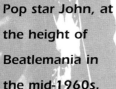

John Lennon was one of the greatest musicians of the 20th century. He came to fame in the 1960s – a decade of great social change. No other public figure summed up the youthful **rebellion** of that era quite so successfully.

John Lennon was the founder and leader of the Beatles – pop music's most successful group. In the Beatles, as one half of the Lennon-McCartney songwriting team, he created an unmatched succession of hit singles which form an unforgettable soundtrack to the 1960s. His solo work in the early 1970s was similarly successful.

Pop star John, at the height of Beatlemania in the mid-1960s.

When he moved to New York in 1971 his music and political activity were considered such a threat to American society that the Republican government of President Richard Nixon spent four years trying to deport him.

By 1977 the political climate in America had changed, and Lennon and wife Yoko Ono were invited to Democratic President Carter's inaugural ball.

This book is to be returned on or before the last date stamped below or you will be charged a fine

Paul Dowswell

Heinemann
LIBRARY

www.heinemann.co.uk

Visit our website to find out more information about **Heinemann Library** books.

To order:

☎ Phone 44 (0) 1865 888066

🖹 Send a fax to 44 (0) 1865 314091

🖥 Visit the Heinemann Bookshop at www.heinemann.co.uk to browse our catalogue and order online.

First published in Great Britain by Heinemann Library, Halley Court, Jordan Hill, Oxford OX2 8EJ, a division of Reed Educational and Professional Publishing Ltd.
Heinemann is a registered trademark of Reed Educational & Professional Publishing Limited.

OXFORD MELBOURNE AUCKLAND JOHANNESBURG BLANTYRE GABORONE IBADAN PORTSMOUTH NH (USA) CHICAGO

Produced for Heinemann Library by Discovery Books Limited
Designed by Barry Dwyer
Originated by Dot Gradations
Printed and bound in Hong Kong/China

ISBN 0 431 08661 3 (hardback)   ISBN 0 431 08662 1 (paperback)
05 04 03 02   05 04 03 02
10 9 8 7 6 5 4 3 2   10 9 8 7 6 5 4 3 2

British Library Cataloguing in Publication Data

Dowswell, Paul
John Lennon. – (Heinemann Profiles)
1. Lennon, John, 1940-1980 – Juvenile literature 2. Beatles — Juvenile
   literature 3. Rock Musicians – Great Britain – Biography – Juvenile
   Literature
I. Title
782.4'2'166'092

Acknowledgements

The Publishers would like to thank the following for permission to reproduce photographs: Camera Press pp6, 11 (Richard Stonehouse), 41 (Elena Adair); Corbis p31 (Henry Diltz); Pictorial Press pp4, 7, 8, 9, 15, 18, 19, 21, 25, 27, 30; Popperfoto pp42, 45; Redferns pp12 (Astrid Kirchherr), 33 & 38 (Tom Hanley), 51 (Elliott Landy); Retna p17; Rex pp5, 16, 20, 23, 28, 35, 36 (and sidebar), 43, 47, 48 (Brian Rasic), 49

Cover photograph reproduced with permission of Pictorial Press

Any words appearing in the text in bold, **like this**, are explained in the Glossary.

The impact of his murder in 1980 was comparable with the death of US President Kennedy in 1963, or Diana, Princess of Wales, in 1997. Millions mourned his passing. For many, he was a cherished symbol of their youth, but for fans young and old he was also an admirable **idealist**, whose work and campaigning for peace stirred consciences and prompted direct action world-wide.

John's death in 1980 prompted scenes of public grieving all over the world. This gathering of fans took place in New York.

To understand why the death of a pop singer should arouse a similar degree of public grief to that of a president or world famous princess, we mainly need to look at John's music. His early Beatles' hits, such as 'A Hard Day's Night,' 'Help!' and 'Nowhere Man' transformed pop with their intimate lyrics and daring melodies. Later Beatles' work, such as 'A Day in the Life' and 'Strawberry Fields Forever' brought an even greater **sophistication** to pop culture. After the Beatles, John released his best known song, 'Imagine'. Many people were moved by its beautiful melody and idealistic sentiment. Other songs from the early 1970s, such as 'Mother' and 'God' remain some of the most powerful and moving works in modern pop music.

Early Years in Liverpool

Bombs rained down on the city of Liverpool on 9 October 1940, the day John Lennon was born. Europe was at war, and Britain's busiest port was a prime target for German aircraft.

John's mother Julia worked in a cinema, showing people to their seats. His father, Alfred, was a seaman on cargo ships. Abroad when John was born, he soon deserted the family completely. Someone who did rush to see the new baby, though, was Julia's sister Mimi. Arriving at Oxford Street Maternity Hospital as soon as he was born, Mimi had run through the bombs, sheltering in doorways to avoid falling **debris** and **shrapnel**.

John with his Aunt Mimi, in the early 1960s. He remained very close to her throughout his life.

Mimi and her husband George Smith had no children of their own. They doted on their tiny nephew, who was such a frequent visitor to their house in Menlove Avenue that it became his second home.

In 1946 Julia met another man she wanted to live with, and

John moved in permanently with Mimi and George. John didn't seem to mind, at least not on the surface, and Julia seemed quite happy to hand over her son to her sister. Mimi remembers her saying, 'You're his real mother. All I did was give birth.'

John was lucky to have such stand-in parents. Mimi adored him, although she was strict. George was a kind and patient man, and John's ally when he had quarrelled with Mimi. They lived comfortably in a pleasant middle-class area of Liverpool.

25 Menlove Avenue, Liverpool – John's childhood home.

AN IMPOSSIBLE CHOICE

John's childhood had its bleak moments too. Once, his father returned and took John to the seaside for a few days, but when Julia came to collect him, Alfred asked John to chose between them. In the terrible scene that followed John chose his father, but when his mother walked out of the room he ran after her in floods of tears. Twenty years later, John angrily told his father how the incident had scarred him deeply: 'Do you know what it does to a child to be asked to choose between his parents? Do you know how it tears him apart, blows his mind?'

John in his Dovedale Primary School uniform.

A REBELLIOUS CHILD

Uncle George taught John to read before he started school, and a love of books stayed with him throughout his life. Richmal Crompton's 'Just William' stories and Lewis Carroll's *Alice in Wonderland* were his childhood favourites. He was musical too. When he was ten George gave him a battered old mouth organ, which he played constantly.

By then, John attended Dovedale Primary School, Liverpool. John's headmaster recognized him as a bright but wilful child. 'This boy's as sharp as a needle,' he said. 'He can do anything, as long as he chooses to.' John did well at primary school and won a place at the local **grammar school** – Quarry Bank.

Aged 11, John had developed into an aggressive child. He was too rebellious to settle at Quarry Bank, and did badly in his studies. There is some evidence to suggest he may have been **dyslexic**, although this wasn't recognized at the time.

When John was fourteen Uncle George died suddenly. John's biographer Ray Coleman reflected: 'In the recurring arguments with Mimi about his lack of discipline, lovely Uncle George had been his mate. They had gone for walks together. He adored the man's gentleness.' But at this terrible time John at least had his mother to comfort him. He had begun to see more of her, and admired her bubbly personality and rebellious nature.

DISCOVERING ELVIS

In his mid–teens he discovered the guitar. Like millions of other British teenagers, John had been spellbound by rock and roll – a new and wildly exciting type of music from America, which he would hear on the radio. Once he heard Elvis Presley singing 'Heartbreak Hotel' he knew this was what he wanted to do with his life. Mimi was not pleased. 'I never got a minute's peace.... In the end I said "Elvis Presley's all very well, John, but I don't want him for breakfast, dinner and tea." '

Like many 1950s' teenagers, John was knocked out by American pop performers such as Elvis Presley.

Despite her misgivings, Mimi bought John a guitar. Julia, who played banjo, taught her son a few chords. John practised so much Mimi banished him to the porch of the house to play.

LIFE WITH THE QUARRYMEN

In 1957 John formed a group with some of his fellow Quarry Bank schoolmates, featuring himself as the lead singer and guitarist. They called themselves the Quarrymen, and began to play at parties and school dances.

One booking, at a summer garden party at St Peter's Church in the Liverpool suburb of Woolton, was to change John's life. In the audience was Paul McCartney. He met the group afterwards, and impressed them with his guitar playing. John was the leader of the Quarrymen and Paul would clearly be competition. But John was clever enough to realize that Paul was too good a talent to pass by. McCartney joined his group, sharing lead vocals, and the spotlight, with John. Paul's friend George Harrison joined soon after. The most important group in the history of pop music had simply fallen into place within the space of a few months.

Double-tracking

John couldn't bear to listen to his own singing voice, which he thought sounded thin. On most of his records his voice is double-tracked (recorded twice) and treated with echo, to thicken it.

*John singing
with the
Quarrymen in
1957. This photo
was taken on the
day John met
Paul McCartney.*

That summer was also John's final year at Quarry Bank. Although he had failed all his exams, Liverpool College of Art were impressed by his cartoons and sketches, and accepted him. It was here that he met Cynthia Powell, a fellow student who was to become his first wife.

FAMILY TRAGEDY

1958 was significant too, but for the worst possible reason. John's mother Julia was killed in a road accident. John remembered the night all too clearly. 'We were sitting waiting for her to come home, wondering why she was so late. The copper [policeman] came to the door to tell us. It was just like… the way it is in the films – asking if I was the son and all that. Then he told us and we went white. It was the worst thing that happened to me.'

The Rise of the Beatles

John bottled up his feelings over Julia's death, but it strengthened his growing friendship with Paul McCartney, who had lost his own mother to cancer two years previously.

A steady stream of bookings for their group kept them busy. Paul and John began to write songs together too. This was mainly so that they would not be playing the same popular hits as other groups they shared a bill with.

A move to Germany

By 1960 they were getting enough work to persuade John that he could make a career in music, and he dropped out of art college. A month later, his

John (right) in Hamburg with fellow Beatles Stuart Sutcliffe (centre) and George Harrison (left).

group travelled to Hamburg. This German port had a thriving night life, and there was plenty of work for English performers who could play rock and roll music. The band had been through various line-up changes and now consisted of John Lennon and Paul McCartney on guitars, George Harrison on lead guitar, John's friend Stuart Sutcliffe on bass, and a drummer called Pete Best. During their time in Hamburg Stuart Sutcliffe left, and Paul switched from guitar to bass. The group also settled on a name – the Beatles.

Hamburg was a tough introduction to show business. The group lived in a filthy flat behind the screen of a local cinema. They played all night to drunken sailors and brawling locals, then collapsed into bed at dawn. It was in Hamburg that they adopted their famous, and soon to be copied, 'moptop' haircuts. For a generation brought up on military-style short hair, the moptop was considered outrageously long.

How the 'Beatles' came to be

The name the 'Beatles' is so familiar it is easy to forget it is actually an awful pun. The insect name was inspired by 50s' pop star Buddy Holly's backing band the 'Crickets'. The misspelling is a pun on 'beat' – 'beat music' was the name given to the tough, rhythmical music the Beatles played.

Hard work in Hamburg

It was in Hamburg that the Beatles became seasoned musicians. As they stood in front of an unresponsive audience, the manager of the venue would shout "Mak show! Mak show!' encouraging them to perform and entertain, as well as sing and play. This constant work night after night gave them the opportunity to create an act that would bring them international fame.

Success in Liverpool

In between extended stays in Hamburg the Beatles returned to play clubs in Liverpool, where they began to build up a loyal and enthusiastic following. By 1961 John had become so well known locally that he was asked to write a weekly column of stories, poems and cartoons for the local music magazine *Mersey Beat*.

A new image

Their Liverpool success brought them to the attention of a local businessman named Brian Epstein. **Flamboyant** and well-connected, Epstein was immediately intrigued by the group. He went to see them at a **venue** called the Cavern, where they played regularly to excited audiences. 'They were fresh and they were honest and had what I thought was a sort of ... star quality. Whatever that is, they had it....' he recalled.

The Beatles in
1962 at an
award ceremony
with *Mersey Beat*
editor Bill Harvey
(far right). New
drummer Ringo
Starr is in the
centre and John
Lennon is second
from right.

Epstein knew the right people, and auditions with several record companies followed. Although one company told him 'Go back to Liverpool, Mr Epstein. Groups with guitars are out,' the group were soon signed to the EMI record label. Epstein was shrewd enough to know that to widen their appeal the group needed a new image. When he met them, the Beatles wore dirty leather stage outfits – a look that was popular in the 1950s. Epstein kitted them out in daringly cut suits, creating an image that was utterly new and startling.

THE FIRST RECORDING

On the eve of their first recording session, Pete Best was replaced on drums by Ringo Starr. All the elements of the extraordinary Beatles' story were now in place. In September 1962 they travelled to London to record their first single with a producer called George Martin. It was a partnership made in heaven and Martin was to produce them brilliantly for their entire career.

MARRIAGE AND FATHERHOOD

A month before they began recording their first single, John Lennon married his girlfriend Cynthia Powell. She was expecting their first child. In 1963 their son Julian was born in Liverpool. At first, both Cynthia and Julian were kept secret from the public. Brian Epstein thought they would be bad for the group's image. It was an awkward start to the marriage, and the fame and fortune that were to follow would only make things worse.

John and his wife Cynthia make a public appearance in the mid-1960s.

First hits

The Beatles' first single, a bouncy song called 'Love Me Do' was not a runaway success. It reached number 17 in the British pop charts. But the follow up, 'Please Please Me,' was something else. A wild, noisy plea to a would-be lover, it climbed to number one in the charts. An album, also called 'Please Please Me,' repeated the single's success. After that, there was no looking back. The next twelve Lennon–McCartney songs went to number one in the British charts.

John and songwriting partner Paul McCartney pose uneasily in their stage gear, prior to a performance.

'Had there been no Beatles … John would have emerged … as a man to be reckoned with. He may not have been a singer or a guitarist, a writer or a painter, but he would have been a Something. You cannot contain a talent like this.'

Beatles' manager Brian Epstein, 1964

WORLD FAMOUS

The Beatles at a press conference in 1963. The Beatles' success with the press was a major factor in their rapid rise to fame.

By the autumn of 1963, television appearances triggered an outbreak of fan **hysteria** the newspapers dubbed 'Beatlemania'. In November, the Beatles played the 'Royal Variety Command Performance' – a British showbiz tradition where popular acts performed to an audience which included the Queen. The event was televised and Lennon quickly established himself in viewers' minds as the rebellious, sharp-witted Beatle. 'On the next number would those in the cheap seats clap their hands? The rest of you, rattle your jewellery,' he quipped.

OFF TO AMERICA

With Britain at their feet, the 'fab four', as the press had dubbed them, headed for America. Here, the

Lennon/McCartney song 'I Want to Hold Your Hand' had already made number one in the national music chart. On 7 February 1964 they stepped out of a plane at JFK airport, New York, to be greeting by thousands of shrieking teenage girls. Driving from the airport into New York City, every single channel they turned to on the car radio was playing a Beatles' record. It was an extraordinary moment, and for the next two years the Beatles could do no wrong. Hit followed hit all over the world. Not only were they massively popular with fans, but serious music critics also loved them. The British newspaper *The Sunday Times* went so far as to describe Lennon and McCartney as 'the greatest composers since Beethoven'.

John features in an American comic from 1964. The caption describes John as the 'Boss Beatle', which he was in their early days.

From Me to You

Explaining how they came to write early hits such as 'She Loves You,' 'From Me to You,' 'Please Please Me' and 'I Want to Hold Your Hand,' Lennon said: 'Paul and I decided not to do anything too complicated. That's why we always included words like "me" and "you" in the titles. It helps listeners identify with the lyrics.'

CASHING IN ON SUCCESS

Their pop fame opened other artistic avenues. The group made two films in 1964 and 1965 – *A Hard Day's Night* and *Help!*, which were both hugely popular. John also had two books published in 1964 and 1965 – *In His Own Write* and *A Spaniard in the Works*. These were collections of poems, drawings and stories and both became instant best-sellers. In

the hysterical worship that surrounded the Beatles, his punning wordplay was compared with the renowned Irish author James Joyce. Now John's books are an all-but-forgotten footnote to his career.

John, his first book in hand, mugs for the camera with fellow Beatles.

FAME BRINGS MEDALS

In June 1965 it was announced that the Beatles were to be awarded Member of the British Empire (MBE) medals, in recognition of the millions of pounds their global success had earned the British record industry. Such public acclaim was usually reserved for distinguished civil servants or high-ranking military men. Many people were shocked, not least the Beatles themselves. John Lennon was bemused.

Being patted on the back by the **establishment** was not something that pleased him. 'I thought you had to drive tanks and win wars to get an MBE,' he quipped.

John (left) and Ringo show the press their MBEs.

The award caused huge controversy. The extracts below, taken from Elizabeth Thomson and David Gutman's book *The Lennon Companion*, show a cross section of opinions, and give a keen insight into social attitudes in the mid–1960s:

'What is the point of serving a country that awards MBEs to a group of young pop singers?'

K S Nash. Letter to *The Times*, 16 June 1965

'What would be the point of serving a country that tried to ignore the talent, vivacity, and even the dollar-earning capacity of its young?'

R I L Guthrie. Letter to *The Times*, 18 June 1965

'They have started a fashion of music making among the young in the street and have made it smarter to tote [carry] a guitar than a cosh [stick or club].'

Charles de Hoghton. Letter to *The Times*, 19 June 1965

'For the next war do not count on me – use the Beatles or the Beatniks.'

Dr Gaetan Jarry. Formerly Royal Canadian Navy. Telegram to the Defence Minister, 21 June 1965

THE BUBBLE BURSTS

But even at the height of his success, John was not happy. Like all the Beatles he felt stifled by their overwhelming fame. In 1966, an honest but careless remark about religion caused a huge controversy. While talking to a journalist, he said: 'Christianity will go. It will vanish and shrink…. We're more popular than Jesus now….' In America the remarks were misinterpreted by certain Christian organizations to mean that Lennon had said that the Beatles were greater than Jesus. Death threats followed, and religious groups held rallies where Beatles' records were burned.

John felt completely humiliated by the fuss he had caused, and the group faced further death threats and bomb hoaxes when they toured America that year. During a performance in Memphis a firecracker exploded in the crowd, and each Beatle looked at the other, wondering who had been shot. They played their last ever gig at Candlestick Park, San Francisco, in August 1966, and vowed never to perform in public again.

UNHAPPINESS AT HOME

At home all was not well either. John had used some of his Beatles' fortune to buy a mansion in the Surrey town of Weybridge, where he lived with

Cynthia and Julian. Two of his songs from this period, 'Help!' and 'Nowhere Man,' are autobiographical. 'Help!' is an admission of his need for support from others, and 'Nowhere Man' is a weary depiction of a secluded, drug-taking existence and a marriage going stale.

Journalist Maureen Cleave's report in the London *Evening Standard* gives a vivid flavour of the aimless, bizarre life John was living at the time. 'One feels that his possessions – to which he adds daily – have got the upper hand; all the tape recorders, the five television sets, the cars, the telephones of which he knows not a single number.'

Cleave finished her report with a quote from John. 'Weybridge won't do it all. I'm just stopping at it, like a bus stop.... All I know is, this isn't *it* for me.'

MEETING YOKO

In the midst of his unhappiness John travelled to London one day to attend an exhibition by Japanese artist Yoko Ono. They met and both felt an instant attraction and fascination. Yoko began to pursue John with single-minded determination, phoning and writing to him regularly.

Although his marriage was slowly falling apart John was still able to make a major contribution to the Beatles' epic album 'Sgt Pepper's Lonely Hearts Club Band,' which was recorded at this time. Its extraordinary final track 'A Day in the Life' is mainly written by John. It was described by **musicologist** Ian MacDonald as '…the peak of the Beatles' achievement. …its musical expression is breathtaking, its structure at once utterly original and completely natural. [It] remains among the most penetrating and **innovative** artistic reflections of its era.'

DIFFERENCES OF OPINION

But just as the Beatles were peaking creatively, their manager Brian Epstein died of an overdose of sleeping pills. Brian had held the Beatles together in a way no one had quite appreciated. After he died their career deteriorated into a mess of ill-advised business deals and bickering.

John and Cynthia (with George Harrison), on a spiritual trip to India in 1968, shortly before their relationship ended.

Managerless, the Beatles decided to set up their own business organization, which they called Apple. They would finance their own projects and make money available to anything that appealed to them.

The venture was a disaster, and soon the Beatles were losing £20,000 a week. Facing financial ruin, the group decided they needed a business manager to help them. John, George and Ringo wanted to use a tough American businessman named Allen Klein. Paul, though, wanted his music business father-in-law Lee Eastman to take the job.

A New Marriage and New Directions

In April 1968, when Cynthia was away on holiday, John invited Yoko over to Weybridge and their love affair began.

The first few months of their relationship flashed by in a haze of newspaper headlines. Cynthia and John divorced, and John and Yoko married in Gibraltar in March 1969. As their partnership blossomed, they made experimental films and music together. Their first musical effort, called 'Two Virgins' was put together the night Yoko first stayed at Weybridge, and featured the two of them stark naked on the cover.

They also made political protests together. Like many people at that time, they felt that America should not be sending troops to fight against **communist** soldiers in Vietnam, and that the British government should not be supporting them.

Their first political gesture was a ceremony 'for peace', where they planted acorns at Coventry Cathedral, which had been destroyed in the Second World War. They also held 'bed-ins' for world peace. This was a novel form of protest which involved John and Yoko lounging around in bed, surrounded by the world's press.

The **tabloid press** were quick to ridicule John and his new partner. The British *Daily Mirror* described him as 'a not inconsiderable talent who seems to have gone completely off his rocker'.

Newly married John and Yoko, at a honeymoon 'bed-in' at the Amsterdam Hilton in 1969.

A SEPARATE MUSICAL LIFE

John was so intensely devoted to Yoko that he insisted on having her with him at all times. This caused great friction at Beatles' recording sessions, and the group began to squabble openly. Disagreements with Paul over Allen Klein also increased the personal tensions between them. In 1969 John began to release singles away from the Beatles, such as 'Give Peace a Chance' and 'Cold Turkey', which was about his struggle against drug addiction.

A POLITICAL PROTEST

While many admired his political activities, others were convinced their former hero had gone mad – especially when he returned his unwanted MBE to Buckingham Palace in protest against British and American involvement in wars in Africa and Asia. His letter to the Queen explained 'Your Majesty, I am returning this MBE in protest against Britain's involvement in the Nigeria-Biafra thing, against our support of America in Vietnam, and against "Cold Turkey" slipping down the charts.'

This last, flippant remark undermined any serious point he was trying to make. But looking back on his political activity in the late '60s and early '70s, shortly before he died, he remarked: 'We felt our duty was … to keep on about peace, until something happened, you know, and it was in the tradition of Gandhi, only with a sense of humour.'

With the Beatles now out of their lives, John and Yoko perform for peace.

'The Beatles ... were destroyed (in Lennon's case quite literally) by their own legend ....When you get to the top, there is nowhere to go but down, but the Beatles could not get down. There they remain, unreachable, frozen, fabulous.'

English poet Philip Larkin,
Observer, 1983.

THE END OF THE BEATLES

Meanwhile the Beatles were lurching to an end. In 1970 they made an album and film called 'Let it Be'. The film, which featured sullen, bickering recording sessions, showed a group in the process of falling apart. Amazingly, they still had it in them to make one last album. It was called 'Abbey Road,' and featured a set of powerful songs as good as anything else they'd recorded. John's standout track was his song 'Come Together'.

But by then squabbles over money, and John's desire to work away from the group were leading to a break up. In April 1970 Paul McCartney was the first to admit that the Beatles were no more. 'I didn't leave the Beatles – the Beatles have left the Beatles, but no one wants to be the one to say the party's over,' he told the press.

THE SWINGING SIXTIES

The 1960s are seen by many people as a golden era, and the Beatles' music has become the soundtrack to this extraordinary time. After the continued hardships of the dreary post-war 1950s, Britain was finally able, in the 1960s, to shake off the economic ravages of the Second World War. For a while, the country led the world in music and fashion. The Beatles' music, with its feeling of boundless optimism, love and peace, chimed in well with the times.

It was a wonderful time to be young. Jobs were easy to come by, and young people had more money than ever before. This created a massive market for entertainment, and made the fortunes of the Beatles and many other pop groups.

Wearing their finest psychedelic clothes, the Beatles publicize their album 'Sgt Pepper's Lonely Hearts Club Band'.

Throughout the world social attitudes to sex, class and other areas of society were changing, especially among young people. Young idealists really believed they could change the world for the better, and that rock music would carry this message to the people.

Young people in the 1960s dressed and behaved in a way that many older people found outrageous.

By taking a strong and vocal stance on political problems such as the Vietnam War and **racism** John and the Beatles undoubtedly influenced the way their fans thought about these issues. They made it seem reasonable that mere entertainers should voice the social and political concerns of their **peers**.

'If you want to know about the Sixties, play the music of the Beatles.'
                    American composer Aaron Copland

'Far away from us on the other side of the sun-flooded chasm of the Sixties, the Beatles can still be heard singing their buoyant, poignant, hopeful, love-advocating songs.'
                    Ian MacDonald. *Revolution in the Head*, 1994

LIFE WITH YOKO

With the split out in the open, relations between the two most successful songwriters of the century soured. The depth of their bitterness, over Klein, over Yoko, over the break up of the group, soon became plain to see. Paul adopted the position of hurt, innocent party, and continued to insist he loved John. John on the other hand gave the cruel side of his character free-rein, taunting Paul, who he dismissed as a lightweight talent and a 'straight' – slang at the time for someone who was boringly conventional in their attitudes.

A SUCCESSFUL SOLO CAREER

In the wake of the split John continued to throw himself into his work, and his public and artistic profile remained high. Still trying to rid himself of the hurt and rejection of his childhood he tried a form of **psychoanalysis** called '**primal** therapy'. In this treatment the patient is encouraged to relive his most painful memories, and relieve his anger and hurt in a fit of screaming. The treatment had a major influence on his next album. Called 'Plastic Ono Band' it was to be the artistic high point of his solo career.

Sparsely produced with just drums, bass and John on piano and guitar, the recording opens with the

haunting 'Mother,' a hymn to Julia and a rebuke to his still living father. Another track on the album, entitled 'God', is an extraordinary rejection of his past and all the Sixties fashions the Beatles and the whole **hippy** culture had championed. 'The dream is over,' sang John to his hippy fans, telling them he felt the ideals of the 1960s were dead.

Seven months later John spent seven days recording his most successful post-Beatles album 'Imagine'. The title track was to become a world-famous anthem. The album also contained 'How Do You Sleep?' a scathing and blatantly unfair attack on Paul McCartney. Irrational it may have been, but it certainly illustrated the level of anger John felt towards his former partner.

MIXING POLITICS AND MUSIC

In July 1971 John told a press conference: 'In England I'm regarded as the guy who won the **pools**. [Yoko's] regarded as the lucky Jap who married the guy who won the pools. In America we are both treated as artists.' Less than two months later, they left the UK for America.

Settling in New York, John and Yoko continued their involvement in politics with both financial help and public appearances. 'Some Time in New York City,' an album from 1972, is full of songs inspired by the Lennons' political activity.

John and Yoko's support for campaigns highlighting **civil rights**, **cannabis legalization**, British policy in Northern Ireland and American involvement in Vietnam won them both admirers and enemies. The United States government saw John Lennon as an 'undesirable alien', and decided to deport him.

Sing all about it!

John described his political songs as 'newspaper songs'. He said they were '... when you write about something instant that's going on right now. "Power to the People" and "Give Peace a Chance" are newspaper songs. That's what my job is ... to write for the people now.'

John and Yoko were to spend the next four years locked in legal battles to prevent this happening.

A RIFT WITH YOKO

Their constant togetherness, the public hostility Yoko provoked, and the constant glare of the spotlight they lived their lives under, caused a rift between Yoko and John. In 1973 they separated, and John moved to Los Angeles for a spree of wild living, and a passionate affair with May Pang, one of John and Yoko's assistants. During this time, a distressed Yoko met Paul and Linda McCartney in London. In an extraordinary show of goodwill, Paul and Linda met John when they were in Los Angeles and managed to pave the way towards a **reconciliation** between him and Yoko.

John with his new partner May Pang, a former assistant of John and Yoko's.

LYING LOW

John returned to Yoko in January 1975. He moved back into a building called the Dakota, overlooking New York's Central Park, where they had bought an apartment two years previously. Within weeks Yoko was pregnant. Shortly before the baby arrived, they were told that their four year battle to stay in the USA was over. John was now free to live in New York for as long as he liked.

On 9 October 1975, Yoko gave birth to her and John's only child. John and Yoko named the child Sean, and the couple asked their friend, English rock star Elton John, to be his godfather.

John's last public appearance. He joined Elton John's band on stage in New York in 1974.

A DEVOTED FATHER

With the arrival of Sean, John Lennon decided to retire from public life and devote himself to being a parent. The absence of his own father from his childhood had caused him much grief. When he lived with Cynthia, he was away so much touring with the Beatles, that his own son Julian barely recognized him when he came home. Yoko too, felt John should be Sean's main carer, while she took command of the family finances.

So, after 15 years of living in the limelight, John Lennon retired to bring up Sean, and live a private 'normal' life. By all accounts father and son had a close and loving relationship.

How John coped with the rest of his life during this period is a muddy area. Some biographies paint a picture of a happy and loving house-husband, baking bread, struggling with the cooking, and taking well-earned breaks in a cosy Italian café near the Dakota building. Other accounts depict John as listless, drug dependent and depressed, in a destructive and dead-end relationship with his wife.

With so many conflicting accounts, it is difficult to know where the truth really lies. Perhaps there is some substance in every strand of the story?

Easy money

Whatever the truth, while John laid low and looked after Sean, Yoko managed the couple's finances. The Beatles, and his solo career, had left John a very rich man. Yoko invested this money in various properties, including more apartments in the Dakota, four farms, two yachts, and a collection of works of art. She had a brilliant eye for a good investment, and the Lennon fortune continued to grow.

During this time the battles over the Beatles' income had also been settled and John and Paul McCartney had become friends again, although there was one well-reported occasion when Paul turned up unannounced. John turned him away, saying he was busy looking after the baby.

The relationship with Yoko

Throughout her time with John, Yoko Ono attracted an extraordinary level of hostility. Her experimental art baffled all but the most ardent critics, and her screeching singing style had an equally limited appeal. Despite all the other factors, she was still seen as 'the woman who had broken up the Beatles', and was blamed for John's more **eccentric** political activities.

But perhaps John's relationship with Yoko actually saved his life. Before he met her, his despondent

John and Yoko. As well as being his wife, Yoko replaced Paul as John's creative partner.

state of mind and reckless drug abuse had marked him out as a prime candidate for death or madness. Yoko undoubtedly brought him a great deal of comfort and happiness. John's pet name for her was 'Mother', and she offered him a degree of love and security that he had once craved from his absent natural mother.

> Throughout his life [Lennon] charged restlessly from one idea or person to another, picking up then discarding friends, lovers, gurus, therapists, charlatans, drugs, political stances, until finally, in Yoko Ono, he found, in his own words "The One".'
>
> Lloyd Rose. 'Long Gone John.'
> *Boston Phoenix,* December 1985.

THE LAST MONTHS

'Life begins at forty, so they promise. I believe it, too. I feel fine. It's like twenty-one, and saying: "Wow, what's gonna happen?"'

John Lennon, 1980.

The year 1980 began with a trip to Bermuda on John's yacht *Isis*. During his time as a house-husband, John had taken occasional trips away on his own, which he found invigorating. In Bermuda he launched into a flurry of songwriting activity and decided that now was the time to return to his day job.

A JOINT ALBUM

Back in New York he and Yoko recruited the best musicians they could find and began to record. The plan was to finance the album themselves, and then offer it to whichever record company made them the best deal.

They called the resulting album 'Double Fantasy', after a flower John had seen in Bermuda. It was half John's material, and half Yoko's, and is a heart-on-sleeve celebration of John and Yoko's love for each other and their son Sean.

Such was his status as a rock star, that John's comeback was marked by global media interest. The album sold well, but had a mixed reception from music critics. Writing in the *New Musical Express*, Charles Shaar Murray said: ' "Double Fantasy" is … a fantasy made for two (with a little cot at the end of the bed). It sounds like a great life but it makes for a lousy record. I wish that Lennon had kept his big happy trap shut until he had something to say that was even vaguely relevant to those of us not married to Yoko Ono.'

That December, John seemed on top of the world. Encouraged by his return to the spotlight and by the huge interest that greeted him, he was already at work on a new album.

A family snapshot of the Lennons with son Sean, taken in 1980.

DEATH IN NEW YORK

On 8 December 1980 John and Yoko returned to the Dakota after an afternoon in the recording studio. Lurking in the shadows was Mark Chapman, a fan who had approached him earlier that day to ask for an autograph. Chapman called out 'Mr Lennon!' When John turned, Chapman shot him five times at close range. Then he took out a copy of J D Salinger's *The Catcher In The Rye* and read it while he waited to be arrested.

Lennon signs an autograph for assassin Mark Chapman, a few hours before Chapman shot him.

The police were on the scene in two minutes. They bundled John into a car and rushed him to the Roosevelt Hospital, half a mile from the Dakota. But he died on the way.

Mad or bad?

Many Lennon fans regarded their hero as a saint-like figure. Mark Chapman was obsessed with the former Beatle, and he decided to kill him because he felt he had not lived up to the ideal he worshipped. When Chapman was arrested he told police: 'I've got a big man inside me and I've got a little man inside me. The little man is the man who pulled the trigger.'

SHOCK AROUND THE WORLD

The whole world was shocked by the murder, and heartfelt tributes were published and broadcast over the next few days. As the news broke, fans gathered in spots in the UK and USA that had special significance to the former Beatle, such as Menlove Avenue, the Liverpool College of Art, and especially, the Dakota building in New York. Everyone, it seems, was affected by John's death. Many of those who stood in silent tribute were teenagers – born after the Beatles had become global stars.

Immediately after the murder, fans flocked to the Dakota with flowers.

Yoko and Sean grieve

For Yoko, shocked and grieving in the Dakota, the messages of sympathy that arrived in the thousands brought some comfort. But the presence of the fans outside was an added burden. Some shouted for her to show herself at the window, and others played John Lennon music on radios and cassettes, 24 hours of the day.

'I told Sean what had happened. I showed him the picture of his father on the cover of the paper and explained the situation. I took Sean to the spot where John lay after he was shot.... Sean cried later. He also said, "Now Daddy is part of God. I guess when you die you become much more bigger because you're part of everything." I don't have much more to add to Sean's statement ... Love, Yoko and Sean.'

Yoko Ono in a statement to the world's press two days after John's death.

Mourning a lost dream?

Some felt the massive outpouring of public grief, the endless radio plays of Lennon songs, and the constant stream of newspaper and TV tributes, were out of proportion to John's importance. Perhaps it was a vivid symbol of their own youth and an idealized image of a long gone decade that people were really mourning. American rock critic Lester

Following John's death, protesters highlight the easy availability of hand guns In the United States.

Bangs wrote: 'I don't know which is more pathetic, the people of my generation who refuse to let their 1960s' **adolescence** die a natural death, or the younger ones who will snatch and gobble any shred, any scrap of a dream that someone declared over ten years ago.'

John would have sympathized. When the world's first rock superstar, Elvis Presley, died in 1977, John's friend Elliot Mintz was visibly moved by his death. John was curtly dismissive: 'Don't talk to me about Elvis,' he said. 'He's dead. Don't try to sell me on the dreams and myths of these people.... It's unhealthy to live through anybody.'

THE LENNON LEGACY

'He showed at all times great courage and indifference to mockery, but what he wanted – peace, goodwill, love – remain as elusive as ever. …his lasting value is in his music both before and after the Beatles broke up. Here he was both tough and tender, exact and universal, funny and tragic. Nothing he hoped for came about: wars rage, people hate … yet everyone, it seems, feels diminished by his death.'

Jazz singer George Melly, *Punch* Magazine, 1980.

John's death pushed his commercial and public profile into orbit. His Beatles' and solo albums sold in greater quantities than ever. The songwriting and recording **royalties** he made now flooded in to the Lennon bank account at $150,000 a day.

Some people felt that his death made him more famous than he really deserved, but it is hard to argue that this is the case. Along with Paul McCartney he was one of the most successful performers and songwriters of the century. McCartney continued to have huge success both as a writer and performer outside of the Beatles, and there is no reason to think that someone of John's huge talent, and massive profile, would not have enjoyed similar success.

A flood of records, articles, musicals, books and programmes honouring John's life were produced throughout the 1980s. Among many other tributes, a memorial garden in Central Park, New York, called Strawberry Fields, was built in his memory.

The darker side of Lennon

John's sons Julian and Sean in 1984. Both would follow their father and become musicians.

But there were other, more unpleasant events and memorials. Diaries and other personal possessions were stolen from the Dakota by former friends or employees. The adoration John's death evoked also provoked opposition and a public appetite for gossip about John's darker side. Albert Goldman's biography *The Lives of John Lennon* was one of many books and articles which showed that John could be a highly dislikable man.

After 10 years of relentless exposure, John's appeal also appeared to be waning. Planned memorial concerts to mark the tenth anniversary of his death were poorly attended or cancelled, although a Lennon tribute in Japan attracted 78,000 visitors.

INSPIRING OTHER MUSICIANS

From the early 1960s to the present day, many musicians have been inspired by Lennon and the music he made, both on his own and with the Beatles. The Beatles' unique mixture of American **blues** and country music, and British hymn and music hall tunes changed the sound of pop music. The lyrics John and Paul wrote broadened the standard pop theme of boy meets girl to take on deeper themes such as social discontent, the generation gap, **surrealism** and drugs.

The 'Anthology' series of unreleased Beatle material came out in 1995, and showed that Lennon and the Beatles were as popular as ever.

Many young musicians today are still inspired by John Lennon and his music. There could be no clearer example of his continuing influence than Liam Gallagher, singer in the British group Oasis, naming his first child Lennon.

THE MUSICAL LEGACY

In the mid-1990s, the surviving Beatles got together to promote their **out-takes** and **demo versions** collection *Anthology* 1, 2, and 3. They also played on two unreleased Lennon songs called 'Real Love' and 'Free as a Bird', which were

THE ROCK AND ROLL HALL OF FAME®   TH

Paul McCartney poses with Yoko and Sean Lennon in 1994, on the day McCartney inducted John Lennon into the 'Rock and Roll Hall of Fame'.

released as singles. Their success, and that of a *Live at the BBC* recording, confirm that John Lennon and the Beatles were the most successful and enduring recording group of the 20th century.

In the early 21st century, the music of John Lennon and the Beatles still fills the 'B' section of record shop counters throughout the world. Their albums are endlessly recycled in CD, mini disc, or whatever new format the music industry devises. These recordings still sell at full price, although some were made nearly 40 years ago. For many, Lennon and the Beatles remain a cherished and unforgettable reminder of the 1960s. To some younger people today, their music evokes a more exciting, colourful age. For fans young and old, John Lennon is still the ultimate political rock musician and people's pop star.

CHANGING VIEWS OF JOHN LENNON

'I'm John and I play the guitar. Sometimes I play the fool.'

John Lennon on the Beatles' CD *Live at the BBC*

'I always was a rebel. On the other hand I wanna be loved and accepted and not be this loud-mouthed lunatic poet musician. But I cannot be what I'm not.'

John Lennon

'Some artists don't suffer fools gladly. John never suffered them at all.'

Jimmy Tarbuck. School friend, and entertainer

'He was a terrible guy, actually, but I liked him.'

Liverpool student friend

'My guess is that Lennon and McCartney will still be remembered when most of our "modern composers" are forgotten by everyone except musical historians.'

Ned Rorem. 'The Music of the Beatles'.
New York Review of Books, January 1968.

The man who gave peace a chance. The house-husband. The feminist. The father. The political activist. The drunk during a fifteen-month spree, separated from his wife. The philanderer. The arrogant swine with a heart of gold. Analysing the aspects of Lennon's character has never presented a simple solution.'
Ray Coleman. *Lennon: The Definitive Biography*, 1984.

'John spent the better part of his life trying to improve himself as a human being, evolving from a physically aggressive youth into a man of peace, from a chauvinist to a house-husband.'
Richard Buskin. *The Complete Idiot's Guide to The Beatles*, 1998.

'Until Lennon, rock 'n' roll had rarely been so abrasive, confessional, otherworldly, primal, political or so deeply moving and thought-provoking (and certainly never all at once).'
Tom Doyle. '100 Greatest Stars of the 20th Century'.
Q Magazine, August 1999.

John's fame, ready wit and political opinions ensured that the world's press would always be interested in what he had to say.

FILMS, BOOKS AND RECORDS

FILMS

1964	*A Hard Day's Night*
1965	*Help!*
1966	*How I Won the War*
1967	*Magical Mystery Tour*
1968	*Yellow Submarine*
1970	*Let it Be*
1988	*Imagine: John Lennon*

The 1994 film *Backbeat* is a creditable dramatization of the Beatles' pre-fame years.

BOOKS

1964	*In His Own Write*
1965	*A Spaniard in the Works*

RECORDS

Beatles' singles

1962
'Love Me Do'

1963
'Please Please Me'
'From Me to You'
'She Loves You'
'I Want to Hold Your Hand'

1964
'Can't Buy Me Love'
'A Hard Day's Night'
'I Feel Fine'

1965
'Ticket to Ride'
'Help!'
'We Can Work it Out'

1966
'Nowhere Man'
'Paperback Writer'
'Eleanor Rigby/Yellow Submarine'

1967
'Strawberry Fields Forever/
    Penny Lane'
'All You Need Is Love'
'Hello Goodbye'

1969
'Get Back'
'The Ballad of John and Yoko'

1970
'The Long and Winding Road'

1995
'Free as a Bird'
'Real Love'

Beatles' albums

1963
'Please Please Me'
'With the Beatles'

1964
'A Hard Day's Night'
'Beatles for Sale'

1965
'Help!'
'Rubber Soul'

1966
'Revolver'

1967
'Sgt Pepper's Lonely Hearts
    Club Band'
1968
'The Beatles'
1969
'Yellow Submarine'
'Abbey Road'
1970
'Let It Be'
1994
'The Beatles   Live at the BBC'
1995
'The Beatles Anthology 1'
1996
'The Beatles Anthology 2'
'The Beatles Anthology 3'

As a solo artist and with
    Yoko Ono
Singles

1969
'Give Peace a Chance'
'Cold Turkey'
1970
'Instant Karma! (We All Shine On)'
1971
'Power to the People'
'Imagine'
'Happy Xmas (War Is Over)'
1973
'Mind Games'
1974
'Whatever Gets You thru the Night'
'No. 9 Dream'
1975
'Stand by Me'
1980
'Just Like Starting Over'

1981
'Woman'
'Watching the Wheels'
1984
'Nobody Told Me'
1988
'Imagine: John Lennon'

Albums

1968
'Unfinished Music No.1: Two Virgins'
1969
'Unfinished Music No. 2: Life with
    the Lions'
'The Plastic Ono Band – Live Peace
    in Toronto'
'The Wedding Album'
'John Lennon/Plastic Ono Band'
1971
'Imagine'
1972
'Some Time in New York City'
1973
'Mind Games'
1974
'Walls and Bridges'
1975
'Rock 'n' Roll'
'Shaved Fish'
1980
'Double Fantasy'
1982
'The John Lennon Collection'
1984
'Milk and Honey'
1990
'Lennon' (Four CD boxed set)

GLOSSARY

adolescence the stage in a person's life between the beginning of sexual maturity and adulthood, usually the teenage years

blues a form of black American folk music

cannabis legalization establishing laws to allow the taking of the drug cannabis

civil rights personal rights, which are supposed to be upheld by law, such as the right to vote, and equal treatment regardless of race

communist some one who believes in communism – a political doctrine in which the state controls the wealth and industry of a country on behalf of the people

debris fragments of something that has been destroyed – such as a building blown up by a bomb

demo version a musical term meaning a rough trial recording

dyslexic unable to read letters correctly

eccentric behaving in a bizarre and unconventional manner

establishment the section of society which controls the government, army, church and civil service

flamboyant extravagant or boisterous in colour or behaviour

grammar school a British secondary school where pupils are generally expected to go to university or other kinds of higher education

hippy a 1960s' term for someone with long hair and flamboyant clothing, whose lifestyle differed from that of mainstream society.

hysteria a frenzied emotional state, especially uncontrollable crying, screaming or laughing

idealist a person who strives for, and expects, the best in human behaviour, both in themselves and other people

innovative something which has never been done before

musicologist someone who studies music in a detailed and analytical way

out-takes left-over recordings of songs which are not released on an album

peers people of the same age or status

pools a British form of gambling where people try to guess the results of football matches in order to win money

primal fundamental, basic

psychedelic something, especially music, clothes or art, that has been influenced by hallucinogenic drugs

psychoanalysis a medical technique for treating mental and emotional problems

racism prejudice against, or hatred of, a person based on their racial group

rebellion opposition, often angry or violent, towards authority

reconciliation when enemies agree to become friends

royalties money paid by a record company for sales of an artist's recordings

shrapnel fragments of an exploding bomb

sophistication cleverness and complexity

surrealism a form of art characterised by strange, often dream-like images

tabloid press newspapers which generally concentrate on the more sensational and lurid aspects of events

venue a place where concerts take place

INDEX

Beatlemania 18–19

Beatles 4, 12, 13–22, 24–25, 27, 29, 30–31, 48–49

Bermuda 40

Best, Pete 13, 16

Cavern, the 14

Chapman, Mark 42

Coventry Cathedral 26

Dakota building, New York 36, 38, 42, 43

death 5, 42–45

double-tracking 10

Dovedale Primary School, Liverpool 8

drug abuse 23, 27, 37, 39

Eastman, Lee 25

Epstein, Brian 14–15, 16, 23, 24

Gallagher, Liam 48

Gibraltar 26

Hamburg 13–14

Harrison, George 10, 12, 13, 25

India 25

John, Elton 36

Klein, Allen 25, 27

Lennon, Alfred 6, 7

Lennon, Julia 6–7, 9, 11

Lennon, Julian 16, 23, 37, 47

Lennon, Sean 36–37, 41, 44, 47, 49

Liverpool 6–7, 8, 10–11, 14

Liverpool College of Art 11, 43

Los Angeles 35

Martin, George 16

MBE 20–21, 28

McCartney, Linda 35

McCartney, Paul 10, 25, 27, 29, 32, 33, 35, 38, 49

as songwriting partner 12–13, 17, 46

Memphis 22

Menlove Avenue, Liverpool 6–7, 43

Mersey Beat 14, 15

New York 4, 34, 36–37, 42–43, 47

Ono, Yoko 4, 24, 26–28, 34–42, 44, 49

Pang, May 35

political protests 26, 28, 31, 34–35

Powell, Cynthia 11, 16, 23, 25, 26

Presley, Elvis 9, 45

Quarry Bank School, Liverpool 8, 11

Quarrymen 10–11, 12–13

Royal Variety Command Performance 18

San Francisco 22

Smith, George 6–7, 8–9

Smith, Mimi 6–7, 8–9

Starr, Ringo 15, 16, 21, 25

Sutcliffe, Stuart 12, 13

Swinging Sixties 30–31

USA 18–19, 22, 34–37

Vietnam War 26, 28, 31, 34

Weybridge 22–23, 26